CHANGE THE TIRE

Correcting, Communicating and Continuing Culture

ZACHARY BREWSTER SR.

Copyright 2018 Zachary Brewster Sr.

No part of this book may be reproduced in any written, electronic, recording, or photocopying without written permission of the publisher or author. The exception would be in the case of brief quotations embodied in the critical articles or reviews and pages where permission is specifically granted by the publisher or author.

Printed in the United States of America

Paperback ISBN:9781979177474

Hardcover ISBN:

www.JETLAUNCH.net

CONTENTS

1. Dealing with Deflation 1
2. Acknowledging the Need for Assistance ... 8
3. The Real Problem 15
4. Incremental Improvement 22
5. Rotating......................... 33
6. Balancing........................ 42
7. Alignment 49

CHAPTER 1

DEALING WITH DEFLATION

5:45 a.m.! Just like every other Monday morning, my alarm echoes through the entire house but is seemingly only programmed for my ears. Roll out of bed, hit the bathroom, shorts and sneakers on, tiptoe out of the bedroom and down the stairs to ensure that no one's REM sleep is interrupted. Left out of the driveway and three miles I go through my neighborhood, on a pace that has me back home and in the shower by 6:30 a.m. Otherwise, my wife beats me to it and my whole day is thrown off.

Whew, I made it! After my shower, I am prepared for what I call the daily dance. Do-si-do with my seven-year-old daughter who always enters the room without knocking right before I put my pants on, which causes me to yell "Wait!" The Electric Slide with my wife, who is constantly switching from one side of the vanity to the other for blow dryers, lipstick, makeup, etc. The Wobble through the mound of toys my

Chapter 1

three-year-old son is sure to have left on the floor to ensure my short-term disability policy is never cancelled. The Cupid Shuffle, with my 13-year-old daughter—and with her it's that I potentially require she make a wardrobe change or that she's refusing to face anyone at school—rounds out my morning.

Once I make it through the Daily Dance, then it's a dash to the garage by 7:22 a.m. in hopes I beat morning traffic. This is especially tricky with my wife constantly saying, "Ted, don't forget…" a thousand things. I'm sure to drop the ball at some point during the course of my day. Out of the driveway, ESPN radio on, through the school traffic and to the freeway to make it into the office by 8 a.m.

Although my weekdays seem routine, they never are, because factors can change at any time. In the car, like clockwork, my mom calls at 7:45. "Eddie, did you sleep well last night?" What she really means is did I get a full eight hours because she's convinced if I don't I won't live another day. Of course, she's the only person in my life who still calls me Eddie. It's because I'm a Jr., and it doesn't bother me at all. As it stands, I currently have four names I answer to. Since my company hired a new CEO, Ted Edwards, my coworkers call me by my middle name, Andrew. The new aforementioned CEO calls everyone by their last name, so besides answering to Ted, Eddie, and Andrew, I also answer to Mills. I can hear him now, as he meets with all the VPs today, "Mills, how are we doing with sales?"

As I juggle my mom's call, attempt to hear what Fantasy Football insiders recommend for tonight's game, as well as navigate through traffic and mentally prepare for what's called the "Motivational Monday Meeting," I hear a sound you never want to hear, especially on the highway.

As if to confirm what I think I hear, my steering wheel begins to shake and the sensors on my dashboard light up. It's 7:48 a.m., and I have a flat tire. I'm seven minutes from getting off my exit and into my parking spot, which always gives me five minutes to get up the elevator and drop my bag in my office to be in my chair my 7:59 a.m.

Of course, no one want to hear, *"Mills, so glad that you could join us."* So now I have to hop out and find the spare, which I have never physically seen and get this thing changed like a NASCAR pit crew to have any hope of even making the meeting at all. Furthermore, I need to make sure I'm not killed in the process, as cars race by as if they're going after the checkered flag.

Chapter 1

As I look in the back under the floorboard of my SUV, to discover that the tools are there, but the tire isn't I finally get on the ground in my dress shirt and slacks to find the tire tucked nicely underneath the back of my car. Locating it is one thing, but getting it off and put on is another. I open the glove box and grab the manual, which has never been unwrapped, and begin to thumb through. RING, RING, RING … In all the chaos, I forgot to call the office to tell them about my car, and it's now 8:08 a.m.

"Mills, will you be joining us today?"

"I'll be there as soon as possible, sir. Please forgive me for not calling, I've unfortunately had a flat tire and am trying to figure out how to change it and—"

"Mills, we're in the middle of our meeting so I must go now. Let's just hope your sales report isn't flat as well, all the best."

CLICK.

I can't believe he cut me off or that he hung up on me in the middle of our conversation.

Is this what "Motivational Monday" is all about. One of your employees has a flat tire in the middle of the freeway and is out here fighting for his life and trying to get the tire changed to get to your meeting and all you can say is, *"Let's just hope your sales report isn't flat as well"*

I'm so sick and tired of giving 110 percent to this company to be treated like I don't even matter. Where was I for my son's first birthday, on a plane for the company. Where was I when my seven-year-old received her perfect attendance award, absent because I was at a "critical" meeting. Where was I for my daughters eighth grade dance this year, I was filling in for my boss at the Chamber of Commerce dinner so he and his wife could go to Italy!

RING.

"Hello?"

"Ted I called your office, and they said you weren't there."

"I'm on the side of the road, honey. Yeah, everything is fine, I just have a flat. I know I don't sound good. It's because of what Ted Edwards just said to me. Can you believe he cut me off while I was explaining why I wasn't there and said, *'Let's just hope your sales report isn't flat as well?'*

Chapter 1

"The nerve of this guy! I know I need to calm down, but this is what I've been saying to you for the last 18 months, I cannot outsell a bad culture. And no matter how many coin phrases or acronyms he develops, it doesn't change the fact that the culture of our company is broken. As a result, my numbers suffer, because everyone in the organization is simply doing just enough not to be yelled at or criticized, but no one is motivated to give their best efforts.

"Even the Leadership of the company isn't bought into what we say the vision and the mission of the company is, and it's moments like this that remind me of why. And I know you're going to say I sound like a broken record but, honey, it's true. I'm convinced we don't even know what culture is. We think we can shape and change culture by catchy meetings like: 'Motivational Mondays,' 'Team Tuesdays,' 'Winning Wednesdays,' 'Follow Through Thursdays' and 'Finish Strong Fridays,' while the whole time no one even knows why or what we do!

"I bet if you asked one person from each department to recite our mission and vision statement on the spot for a chance for the entire company to get a $10,000 bonus that we wouldn't even come close. Don't even mention our core values or our goals for this year.

"I know I say this stuff all the time, honey, but I'm just exhausted with how we operate. I just wish he would even acknowledge the true definition of culture, because I know that if he focused on it, he'd see the same issues I see and begin the process of bringing about change.

"Ok, yeah, at this point, I'm going to just bite the bullet and call roadside assistance and wait. Love you too!"

What I Want You to Know:

- Culture is a set of shared attitudes, values, goals, and practices that characterizes an institution or organization.
- As a leader, every action and reaction affects the culture of your company.
- A positive and productive culture is not stumbled upon or discovered; it's thoughtfully created.

CHAPTER 2

ACKNOWLEDGING THE NEED FOR ASSISTANCE

Waiting for roadside assistance is like watching the sands of an hourglass. It does, however, give you time to think.

I sit replaying my boss's comment in my mind. How am I supposed to be motivated on a Monday or any other day, if my boss values a meeting over my well-being?

This really frustrates me because I sit and watch this flow through the company and since he's taken over, there's been a shift in everyone's attitude. No one says good morning anymore, no one asks how the kids are doing, no one goes to lunch together. Everyone has his or her head down chasing mind-numbing reports that don't really tell us anything.

The truth is this problem is too big for us to deal with ourselves. We think we can figure it all out by attempting to create all of these themed day initiatives, but none of us know exactly how to address our issues with culture.

It's just like my flat tire, there was a time when dealing with this was simple. You get a flat, you hop out of the car, pop the trunk, grab a lug wrench and a jack and change the tire. The spare was always in the same place and you knew exactly what to do. Now, depending on what type of car you have, the spare could be anywhere or any size. Some of them are still in the trunk, others are under the car, and if it's an SUV, some are hanging on the back door. And that's just the tire, finding jacks and lug wrenches is like a scavenger hunt. Then, when you finally do locate them, you need to be a certified ASE mechanic to use them. The same is true for companies.

Over the last 10 years the workforce has drastically changed. In 1995 the workforce looked like this:

- The Greatest Generation: Born before 1928 = 2%
- The Silents: Born 1928 to 1945 = 18%
- Baby Boomers: Born 1946 to 1964 = 49%
- Gen Xers: Born 1965 to 1980 = 31%

- Millennials: Born 1981 to 1997 (who weren't even represented in the workforce because the oldest person in the group would have been 14 years old)

On the contrary, in 2015 the workforce looked like this:

- Millennials: 35%
- Gen Xers: 34%
- Baby Boomers: 29%
- The Silents: 2%

This major shift in the workforce over the last 10 years has found many companies unprepared and unequipped to address an array of challenges that comes with this type of diversity in the workplace.

Communication style, negative stereotypes and cultural expectations are what many companies find as a common denominator in addressing this shift. However, greater than these three is company culture.

The challenge is that with each of these groups now in the workforce together, each of them is looking for something different and hears a different message when a company's culture is being

Acknowledging the Need for Assistance

communicated. Ted Edwards was a legend in his last company, due to his ability to move the company from being a small local company into a national brand.

The difference in his former company and our organization is that everyone was an independent contractor. So although he has proven industry knowledge and business acumen, there's a major difference in having a small team of 25 at corporate vs. having 400 people spread across three floors in one building and 16 offices over eight more states with 2000 employees. And no matter where I travel, the sentiment is the same. There is no shared vision on why we do what we do or who we are as an organization.

As I sit and ponder these frustrations, I look in the mirror and ask what part I've played I've been with the company for eight years and watched this steady decline. When I started, I was excited to have my first director role. It was my second job out of college, and I had gained tons of experience in my former role as a human resources manager. I really loved having the ability to connect with everyone in the organization.

When I joined this company as the director of human resources, the CEO, at that time, had a vision for changing the world one person at a time. I felt we were on that journey during my first four years and then we grew.

Growth through a significant merger can be both exciting and life altering. Two years into the merger, the company decided that HR needed to be outsourced, but they felt my passion and knowledge of the company would make me a perfect fit for the vice president of sales role that was being vacated due to a retirement.

The first six months in the role was phenomenal. I felt like I was externally expressing all the goodwill about our company that I had done internally for so many years. It didn't even feel like sales, it was sharing the truth about a wonderful company.

In the seventh month, our CEO decided to move on, and Ted Edwards was hired. Amid his hiring, the multigenerational workforce was also becoming a very real dilemma for most companies. Due to my previous years in HR, I was invited to and attended many seminars regarding this challenge, however Ted showed no interest.

Over the last 18 months, I have watched our company sit still, while other companies speed past.

We continually lose our best talent, while being unable to find qualified replacements. Once we

Acknowledging the Need for Assistance

finally get a new hire, we don't have any true means of training them so many of our new employees begin their work with us in a spirit of frustration. Many of our offices feel as though there's an "us" and "them" mentality, as it relates to the attention they receive.

We are constantly asked to provide more productivity with less resources. In our leadership meetings, I look around the room and wonder how we'll ever get out of this cycle. Our CEO and two of our other VP's are Baby Boomers. Another VP is a Silent and I'm a Gen Xer.

To make it even more challenging, the one Silent is our VP of Finance and can't seem to think of any reason why anyone would pay a consultant for anything.

The truth is I could have changed my own tire. The manual has a step-by-step process for me to use the tools in the black bag under the floorboard to do the job myself. Although there are many steps, which include: unlocking the spare, winding the spare down on a lever with the jack, placing the jack under the grooves located under the side of the SUV, raising the car to an angle as to remove the tire, but to be sure that it's not too unbalanced, turning the lug nuts counterclockwise, etc. I clearly could have done this all alone.

The difference is that when the roadside assistance representative finally arrives, she won't ever ask to see my manual or my tools. He simply knows exactly what to do and how to do it because he's skilled at quickly addressing flat tires and getting people moving again.

What's clear to me in this moment is that if our company is ever going to navigate the journey necessary to resurrect our shattered culture, we must first acknowledge the need for assistance.

BEEP, BEEP!

Finally, someone nice enough to at least stop and ask if I need help.

What I Want You to Know:

- A broken culture is caused by a series of decisions that ignore the need for culture to be sustained.
- The multigenerational workforce is often a critical factor in the cultural challenges of an organization.
- Once a company's culture is damaged, it's often necessary to ask for assistance to begin the process of repair.

CHAPTER 3

THE REAL PROBLEM

BEEP, BEEP.

A young man pulls over to the side of the road and gets out of his pick-up truck with a black bag. I realize that he's unsure of my need as he's pulling out a pair of yellow jumper cables. "What a bad way to start your morning! I don't mind giving you a jump— I have few minutes to spare!" he says. "Hey Man, thanks for stopping! I wish I could use the jumper cables, but it's not my battery— it's my tire. Roadside assistance is on the way. I know it's hard to see the front passenger tire when you pass by, but again, I appreciate you stopping." "Sure thing!" he says and hops back in his truck.

I notice that traffic begins to slow down as it usually does around this time of the morning.

BEEP, BEEP.

Chapter 3

A bright red sports car pulls up beside me and a seemingly energetic lady leans out of her window. She must be experiencing the type of morning I had before this nightmare! "Good Morning Sir! I have a gas can in my trunk if you need it!" she says. "Hey! No ma'am, I have a gas can and a tank full of gas. It's a flat tire!" Her smile begins to fade as she realizes that she doesn't have what I need. "I'm so sorry. I can't help you with that but I really hope that your day gets better." For a moment, I felt that I had ruined her day because she seemed so eager to do a good deed and I couldn't help her with that. "It's okay! Roadside assistance is on the way but thank you so much! She slightly smiles and begins to roll up her window. I flag her down again, "Oh and ma'am—thank you again! Your actions show me that there really are some good natured people in the world." Her smile brightens and she waves as her window closes.

I turn and look down the lanes of incoming traffic; I hesitantly feel a sense of relief. I see flashing lights—could it finally be my rescue! The wrecker pulls up—older gentleman gets out. I ask, "Are you here from roadside assistance? "

"No Sir. Just happened to see you and figured I could tow you in if you 're waiting for a tow

The Real Problem

truck in this traffic", he responds. I'm hoping the frustration is not settling in on my face as I realize that he is not the relief I requested over an hour ago. "Oh, no, sir, I don't need to be towed. It's a flat tire. Is that something that you could help with? I know I already called someone else, but it's been over an hour, and they still haven't come."

Immediately, I see a Roadside Assistance Service Vehicle approaching. A somewhat scruffy and unhurried man gets out of truck. "Are you Ted Mills?" "Yes, I'm Ted Mills and it's the tire on the front passenger side", I said swiftly (hoping that my tone would speed up his pace).

As I step aside and allow him to change the tire, I can't help but think about how frustrated I am with everything at work. When I think about our culture, it's kind of like what just happened to me with the flat. Everyone wanted to offer me help that I didn't need.

Company's often face similar challenges in that their key performance indicators focus on sales, cost of goods sold, quality and delivery in order to improve profit, rarely do companies truly focus on the common thread throughout all the KPIs, which is culture.

Chapter 3

It's Not the Battery

When the first guy offered me jumper cables, they would have been very effective, if I had no power. However, I had sat in my car listening to the radio and charging my phone the entire time I waited for roadside assistance.

For any company to move towards its goals, it must be powered by a strong salesforce in order to drive revenue. Consequently, it's often the first place a leader focuses on when he notices an issue in the organization.

Studies show that a negative culture can be counterproductive to the bottom line. Companies with a positive culture can expect to outpace their negative counterparts by 19 percent in operating expenses and 28 percent in earnings growth. Thus the idea that more revenue will solve all of a company's problems is like me expecting to fix my flat with a pair of jumper cables.

I'm Not Out of Gas

If it's not sales then it must be the cost of goods sold, right? Companies often figure that their struggles can be resolved by operating more lean. Just like the lady who stopped to offer me gas, companies often figure that lowering costs will fuel their business in a positive direction.

Conversely, a lean journey is supposed to drive continuous improvement that could potentially lead to cost savings and staff optimization. Far too often companies engage their employees in this effort, as a cost-cutting expedition, that ultimately limits and, in many cases, eliminates innovation and productivity. So while a gas can is always a great resource, there was no need for one in my current situation.

Organizations that use this approach typically see the morale of the staff that remains plummet. Additionally, productivity still suffers due to the exhaustion of the workforce.

I Don't Need to be Towed

Addressing issues with company culture doesn't necessarily mean that everything is broken, and thus must be overhauled. The guy with the tow truck was ready to take me in and give me a full diagnostic on my vehicle, but it made no sense to incur the cost of being towed or have the car diagnosed when I knew that the tire was flat.

This isn't to say there aren't other issues with my SUV that could be revealed in the process, but my primary mission today is to get my car moving again so I know exactly where I have to focus.

Chapter 3

Most companies survey their employees every 12 to 24 months. Across the board, many companies continually see the same themes. Employees feel uninformed of the company's focus, undervalued regarding their work-life balance, untrained in their roles and unclear of their career path with the organization. These issues point to a problem with culture.

The roadside assistance technician changed my tire in 15 minutes. He discovered that there was a nail in the tire that must have caused a slow leak. "Did your sensor not light up and tell you to add air?" he asked. I responded that it only came on today when the tire went flat. "You definitely want to take it in then, because without an indicator of air pressure, you could end up on the side of the road again."

As I crank the car it hit me like a ton of bricks: Businesses that suffer from a flat culture don't experience this overnight, it happens over time. And because we don't have anyone dedicated internally or externally to assist us with shaping and monitoring culture, it was bound to be deflated.

What I Want You to Know:

- Improving your organization should not be limited to increasing profits.
- KPIs are only effective it they are understood and shared by all stakeholders.
- Ignoring culture will leave your company stranded regardless of strong revenue.

CHAPTER 4

INCREMENTAL IMPROVEMENT

It feels great to finally be on the road again, and yet the experience this morning still has me flustered.

How do I go in and face my boss knowing that all he cares about is my sales numbers and not my well-being?

RING, RING, RING.

"Are you supposed to be using your cell phone during school?"

My 13-year-old often calls me when I'm certain she's supposed to be in the middle of a class.

"I understand you're upset with your grade, but I'm not coming to the rescue. If you need more clarity on the assignment and want to ask for an opportunity to submit more work, you're going to have to face her yourself. I'm raising you to be strong and independent, right? I'm glad you said it with me, now stop whining and ask your teacher if you can have a few minutes with her one-on-one. I know it will go well."

As I hang up with my daughter, I get out of my car, grab my bag, dash to the elevator, and make a right turn as the door opens and into my office. No sooner than I get logged into my computer, my phone rings.

"Okay, I'll be over in one second."

As I walk in, he never looks up from his computer.

"Mills, I trust that although you missed the meeting you're prepared to cover your report."

"Yes, sir, I have it right here."

In the middle of reviewing the sales numbers, he stops me and says, "A strong sales pipeline leads to a strong sales performance, and a strong sales performance leads to strong profits." *What about strong people?* I said to myself as he fired off another question. "So, what are we doing to improve these numbers?" I cringed as he asked the question, and before I could answer, he says, "I tell you what, take a half hour and come back with a solution."

Chapter 4

As I walk down the hall, my head is beginning to feel like a bowling ball. I closed my door and turned my chair towards the window for the first five minutes. I must have thought for four and a half of them about how my life would have been different if I had just taken the job I was offered instead of moving into sales.

I'd wanted a new challenge and the opportunity for promotion. If I had only known the expansion would happen and our former CEO would leave. I turned to my computer and began to type a few notes. Twenty-five minutes left. After pulling together all the information I knew he'd want to see, along with calling all my team members and preparing them for what I was going to say, so they'd know what to say when he called to follow up on my report.

With seven minutes left I spun around in my chair, daydreaming again about working somewhere else, my phone rings. "Dad, it worked! I talked to my teacher after class and shared my position and she's going to let me resubmit the whole assignment. She realized she hadn't been clear in her instructions and said that tomorrow she's going to give the whole class another chance. How's that for 'strong and independent,' huh?"

Incremental Improvement

"I'm so proud of you baby! I hate to rush, but I have a meeting in three minutes. Love you!" I all but shout, then grabbed my reports from my desk and headed down the hallway.

When I got to Ted's office his assistant told me to have a seat while he finished up a call. As I sat there I began to realize Ted's and my meetings were always the same. I go in and give him my thoughts, he tells me what they should have been, which is only a regurgitation of what I just said, however when he repeats the same idea to me, it's suddenly an AMAZING DISCOVERY. I leave feeling defeated and frustrated, but I smile because that's what you often are minimized to doing when you meet with your boss. I pretend to agree with what he's saying and if I disagree it's only to the point where he raises his eyebrow or gives an edict that's not based on any strategic thought, other than his title, then I move forward with what he said because he's the boss. And although this is the cycle of most interactions between managers and direct reports, is it right? I couldn't help but hear my own instructions to my daughter. Yet I'm sitting outside of the teacher's office, Afraid to go in and state my feelings about this assignment.

I told her to be strong and independent, but I'm as loose as a Spaghetti Noodle.

Chapter 4

When I enter the office and sit across from him at his conference table and hand him his copy of my report. On page two he stops me and says, "How do you expect to achieve this in the next 90 days based on your current pace?"

His question was related to something on page seven that was explained on page eight. As we turn to page eight for my explanation, he tells me the plan doesn't seem cohesive enough. Never mind that we skipped through the meat of the presentation, where everything he needed to know was explained, he says, "Write this down."

Thirteen minutes later I had a fully revised plan that appeared to be a replica of what I walked in with. "Anything else?" he asked. "No, sir, thanks for your help." To which he replied, "We're a team, Mills, we're a team."

At this point I pushed my chair under the table and headed for the door, but before I placed my hand on the knob, I received a dose of unexpected strength.

"Ted, there is something else." Tentatively I returned to face him. "Yes?" he asked.

"Achieving our sales goals won't address our issues. This company is suffering and it's not because of sales, operations or the days that our invoices are outstanding. And no matter how many 'themed' days we have or costs we cut, our issues will be the same. We pay a premium to have our employees surveyed every 12 to 24 months depending on if finance wants to spend the money. Yet, we take all their responses and treat them like they don't matter. We explain away their feelings of being undervalued by saying that 'no one is ever happy financially.'

Instead of truly addressing training we register them for online courses that aren't integrated into our standard work. We tell them during their orientation that the sky's the limit for their career, but no one can explain where the ceiling is, let alone the sky.

"And when it comes to the company's vision, mission and core values, there's not an employee who can recite it, and the one's that know it can't relate it to how their work makes an impact. This causes us to experience low morale, turnover and a lack of overall quality.

"So, when you ask me how we can improve sales, it won't matter if I land every top account that we desire because our culture is starting to affect how we serve our customers.

Chapter 4

"Frankly, when I first began this role it didn't even feel like sales, because I communicated my passion for a great organization, and our prospects could see it. But now, I have to give myself a pep talk every time I visit an existing or new account in hopes that they won't see my disappointment in what we've become.

"I know that this is a lot, but I may as well get it all out now. When I called you about my flat tire today you said, *"let's just hope your sales report isn't flat as well."* All morning, I've been mulling over this, because it's an illustration of what we've become. You're a brilliant business man, but you've paid so much attention to product, process, planning and profit that you've failed to give any attention to our people.

"I'm so glad I had that flat tire today, because it helped me realize something. If this company doesn't address the real reason why we're stagnant, we'll never improve. While I waited for roadside assistance I had people stopping to offer to give me a boost, gas and even a tow, but none of those things were the issue.

"The issue was that I had a slow leak in my tire that I was unaware of, and it had gotten to a critical point that impacted my ability to drive. I want you to know that I'm committed to the success of our company, but we must address these critical parts.

At this point, Ted's phone rings, which he answers and directs, "Please let them know Mills and I have a meeting that's gone longer than expected and I'll have to reschedule."

That phone ringing felt like my alarm going off at 5:45 a.m. Surely, I had been dreaming and the last 10 minutes of my life had been a dream.

"So Mills, what do you see as the real problem?"

At this point I realize that I'm not in my PJ's and waking up after a night of false heroics, this is REAL.

"The issue is our company culture. All of the things we've been hearing from our employees are clearly linked to our issues with culture, but haven't done anything to address it." By now, I'm knee-deep into this dissertation, so I make my way to the whiteboard in his office. "Just like with my car today, our culture didn't suddenly get this way, and since there's been a clear and steady decline, it's going to take slow and steady improvement.

"In order for this to happen, I really believe we're going to need outside help. This morning,

Chapter 4

I thought I could just jump out and change my tire then get to work but I realized that with newer cars, changing a tire is a major ordeal. And although I could have figured it out, it would have been a long, grueling process that may have done more damage.

"The same is true with culture. It's wise to seek external evaluation and guidance to ensure a positive and productive process. In my opinion, sir, we need a SPARE.

- Seek the assistance of an external consultant.
- Prepare to fully engage in the process.
- Assign an internal champion for the project.
- Relinquish any preconceived notions of the experience.
- Empower the firm we choose to give us transparent criticism.

It seemed like an eternity, as he stared at the acronym I had written on the board.

"Mills, I have to be honest with you, I have never had anyone who works for me share anything with me the way you just did."

Incremental Improvement

At this point I began to brace myself for the two words I had hoped I'd never hear in my career.

"Great Job," he said.

My head jerked. I couldn't believe my ears.

"I'm glad you had the courage to say what you said. I'm calling an emergency VP meeting for 7 a.m. tomorrow morning. I want you to share the same message with the group."

When he stood to shake my hand, I was still a bit numb.

I look forward to the meeting.

When I walked out of the office, his assistant stopped me and said, "You were in there for a long time, Andrew, everything ok?"

I smiled and nodded, but before I could answer, her phone rang, and I could tell it was our boss telling her to arrange our morning meeting. When I got back to my office, I sat in my chair and looked out of the window again. I could see my car and thought about how the day had unfolded.

At 8:08 this morning I was the most frustrated I had ever been. I had a flat tire and was deflated by a comment my boss made about it. And on the same afternoon, there's been a change in both areas.

That conversation with Ted Edwards was just like my spare tire. It's not the end result that I need long-term, but it's enough for me to start the journey.

What I Want You to Know:

- Remaining silent will never change your company's culture.
- Recognizing an issue with culture is the first step to repair it.
- In addressing an issue of culture, consider using a SPARE:

    - **Seek**
    - **Prepare**
    - **Assign**
    - **Relinquish**
    - **Empower**

CHAPTER 5

ROTATING

After work I took my car to the shop. The mechanic took a look at the sensor, and said he'd be able to fix it right away if I had time to wait. I was more than happy to give them all the time they needed to ensure I didn't end up stranded again.

"Mr. Mills? We got ready to patch your tire and realized they hadn't been rotated, balanced or aligned in several miles."

I'm already getting my sensor done and my tire patched, and hope this could wait to the next trip to the mechanic. It seems like mechanics always try to upsell you with additional services, so I'm hesitant to agree to anything.

"You could always wait, but it will affect the performance of your car. Typically, front tires carry most of the car's weight, due to the engine's axle sitting directly over them. When you brake, all of the front brake dust smears the tire. However,

Chapter 5

the issue isn't just cosmetic, although four-wheel drive or all-wheel drive vehicles spread the weight of the car more evenly, approximately 75 percent of a car's weight rests on the front two tires. By not rotating them, tires wear unevenly, causing them to lose tread in the front quicker than they do in the rear."

I couldn't help but think of how the weight of a company is typically distributed. Far too often, the people who are hired to work on the frontlines of a company are left to carry too great of a load and get very dirty in the process. Meanwhile, others, in roles of leadership, are often shielded from the challenges of being in the forefront and are, ultimately, unaware of what the organization is going through. When I started with the firm, everyone, regardless of title, did a rotation. It was meant to ensure that we all knew each other's roles, responsibilities and rigors.

It's often difficult to recreate real pressure when you're in a role for a short period of time that you know will soon end, however, I still remember my time as a receptionist. I couldn't believe the volume of calls that came in each hour. All I could think about was how they ever took a breath or went to the bathroom. When I began my first rotation, I must have witnessed 100 calls in the first 45 minutes, but they all sounded the same.

Rotating

Not that it was the same customer calling or all dealing with the same issue, but the receptionist had the same pleasant tone throughout each call.

At the end of the day I asked what her secret was and she said, "I make the most of every moment." I'm sure that the look on my face showed her that I was interested in hearing more. "I'm committed to answering each call the same way and providing the same service regardless of the nature of the call."

Of course, I chalked her response up to the fact that I was the new HR person, so she clearly wanted to impress me. However, over the next several weeks in each department, I realized each person shared the same sentiments. Not only that, but everyone had a war story about their rotation that became a point of connectivity and a rite of passage throughout the organization.

Unfortunately, we are miles away from where we were, and the tread on our culture is wearing thin. What company's must understand is that culture, the shared attitudes, values, goals and practices that characterize an organization exists whether it's acknowledged or not. Most companies allow culture to take on a life of its on and by the time they recognize the damage, it's too late. The mechanic realized that simply patching my tire's hole wouldn't allow the car to function at its greatest capacity. Thus, he recommended a rotation. I decided to make some notes of how this principle could assist us in correcting our culture.

Recognition

A 2016 Gallup report showed that 87 percent of the employees surveyed lacked motivation and were unhappy. Sadly, even amid numbers like this, many companies attempt to explain away their issues with culture. I feel like Ted Edwards and I had a breakthrough in this area, but it's only the first step. Once they recognize an issue with culture, most organizations either spend a lot of time discussing it with little action, or attempt to address it with very superficial efforts. Recognition is critical, but still only the first step.

Objective

Before culture can be corrected, a clear objective must be determined. The challenge in this area is to neutralize the idea of profit and loss. This can be an exercise in acrobatics, and every business leader worth their salt is trained to drive success towards the bottom line. However, culture is one of those emotional intelligence areas that can be skewed by approaching it with the lenses of dollars and cents.

If the goal of building a solid company culture is limited to an end result of simply increasing net profit, then there will always be a conflict. Regardless of an organizations industry or sector, their culture must be built around why they exist, which is directly linked to what solutions they provide in the marketplace and their competitive differentiators. This core competency of developing vision and mission must be acknowledged when setting the agenda following the initial step of recognition.

Tension

It must be noted that the very nature of this subject brings a level of tension into any company. The question of "How did it get so bad?" and "Who's responsible for perpetuating this problem?" often leads even the most cohesive leadership teams down a path of blame. The goal of acknowledging an issue with culture is not to place the burden on any one person.

In sports, the best athletes in America are those who play after the game has ended. Professional sports commentators are outnumbered by "freelance journalist," who have all the answers. They can detail every pass that should have been thrown, every hit that should have been a homerun, every free throw that should have been made, along with being able to call the game better than the coach. Each of these people work with you wherever you're employed, and, whether you know it or not, they have their own talk shows within your walls. Amongst your leadership team, there is someone who enjoys feeding them insider information, and they are having dialogue about and will continue to discuss your broken culture whether you know it or not. Consequently, when correcting culture, leaders must transparently discuss the impending tension and be prepared to stand together during the process.

Attitude

Reports show that 24 percent of people in the workplace are actively disengaged. Their poll does not rank them by position, so it's safe to assume they're at all levels of the organization. This is alarming because this statistic rates those who show up to work with a poor attitude most the time. When you begin the process of correcting culture, these people will immediately attack your efforts. Unlike those who simply attempt to find fault, these people will attempt to derail the process. Like the tire that went flat, this is a group that needs to be personally patched up prior to the process. In other words, if the mechanic had rotated the flat without a patch, we would still have a major issue.

Target

Contrary to some beliefs, it's very appropriate to begin the process of correcting culture with a numerical goal in mind. There are hundreds of survey tools to measure engagement and overall happiness. As with any SMART goal, you want to ensure you have an attainable expectation.

Imperfections

Each year, company's produce budgets and KPIs that guide their focus. Interestingly, manufacturers also plan for a certain level of product defect, waste and rework. However, most organizations plan the "people" portions of their business with perfection in mind. Even those businesses who measure turnover or off work rates never fully have a true appreciation for the volatility of people. As a result, the journey to correct culture is often met with great consternation as product and process-minded people try to figure out why people "just don't get it." Approaching people with an understanding of our vast diversities helps embrace the patience required for this process.

Offense

In sports, there's a popular saying "offense sells tickets, but defense wins games." When you are starting the journey to correcting the challenges with culture in your company, you need to sell some tickets. This means you must have an approach that people can rally around.

When college football teams want to make a major splash, they go out and they hire a winning coach. The goal is to ignite their fan base and send a message that they're serious about developing a winning culture. The same is true in the business world. Often the best way to show your employees you are willing to do what's necessary to change the environment is to bring in a group of experts, who are equipped in leading the organization to change.

Nuances

Inasmuch as no two people are the same, neither are two companies. Many times the conversation of culture immediately shifts to an organization feeling like they must allow people to bring pets to work or create sleep lounges like at Google or Facebook. Remember, the culture of a company should be directly linked to why they exist and described by their vision, mission and core values, which don't always lend to hacky sack on the front lawn. The key is finding out what fits for you and establishes a healthy environment.

Rotating

The principle of ROTATION is the starting point for addressing an unhealthy culture within an organization. However, there's more to be done to ensure the best performance. The mechanic also explained why my tires needed to be balanced.

What I Want You to Know:

- Addressing one glaring issue doesn't correct culture
- The decision to change company culture is a journey
- Correcting culture begins with ROTATION:

    - **Recognition**
    - **Objective**
    - **Tension**
    - **Attitude**
    - **Target**
    - **Imperfections**
    - **Offense**
    - **Nuances**

CHAPTER 6

BALANCING

I was fortunate to have a very thorough mechanic, so while he was explaining the need for the tires to be rotated, he also explained why they must be balanced. Balancing requires getting the wheels and tires to rotate at high speeds without vibrations. Surprisingly, most wheels and tires aren't perfectly round, even when brand new. What's more, their weight isn't evenly distributed, so in some spots, they're heavier. Either issue can cause annoying vibrations.

Out-of-balance tires can also cause rapid tire or suspension wear, so it's not just about ride comfort. That is why when new tires are mounted on wheels they're spin-balanced to detect vibrations. Some vibrations can be eliminated by rotating the tire on the wheel so the heavy or "high" spot is in a different location that better matches up with the wheel. Small weights are attached to the wheels with adhesives or clips to counteract the heavy spots and provide a smooth ride.

Balancing

As you may have guessed, I related every word he offered to my company's issue with culture. I mean, the principle of rotation is one that involves the leadership team of a company investing their energy in the correction process. But how do you take the next step of involving everyone and communicating culture?

I believe that communicating culture involves the very tedious process of laying out the plan of attack. It's one thing to acknowledge that there's an issue among management, but it's quite another to allow it to permeate down to all people. However, just like my car, I could have simply done the patchwork and the rotation, but that wouldn't ensure I'd have a smooth ride. More than often, companies approach this matter with secrecy vs. transparency, and the true goal of creating a healthy culture is never accomplished. You can't treat a sick patient without informing them of their sickness. An unhealthy organization should be informed of the risks associated with their disease and be given a prescription with specific instructions. I continued making notes using the principle of BALANCE in communicating culture.

Chapter 6

Bridge the Gap between Vision, Mission and Meaning

With only 13 percent of employees engaged at work, it's clear that most organizations haven't figured this out. Thus, a majority of the workforce shows up to work with no clear purpose, which leads to poor performance. Many companies were founded by and are led by remarkable visionaries who crafted elaborate vision and mission statements that have transcended space or time. Regrettably, statistics show that they have also transcended the practical application necessary to create a positive culture. Leaders must be able to communicate why: Why the company was founded; why the company performs a certain way; why there's a positive impact when employees perform well.

Analyze

As important as bridging the gap of vision, mission and meaning is to ensure it's still relevant. It's unadvisable for a company to haphazardly change their vision and mission, but not uncommon to adjust how their work relates. Technology and automation is continually shifting the way companies produce products. Therefore, there is a need to address how the work of the employees relate along the way.

Limitations

During the process of communicating culture, companies must limit the barriers to the access that employees have to senior leaders employees have to senior leaders. Remembering this process is going to have its share of tension, those in middle and frontline leadership must be willing to allow employees to have an active role in the communication of culture. Who better to express the true nature of how the organization is really functioning than those who perform most of the work. No matter how well the leadership of an organization communicates, there's no replacement for firsthand experience. Just like the tires, everyone must accept that no organization is perfectly well-rounded, which is why the process of smoothing out the high spots is critical in balancing. Top leaders must be willing to be leveled out with the organization during this process.

Assign

Once the limitations are removed, a company can then assign champions of this process at all levels. Having a cross-functional group committed to the culture of the company produces the best results. Just like when employees are assigned to tasks based on their technical skills and training, the same is true for culture. Those assigned to this work must have high EQ. These are the people who never meet a stranger and are willing to build relationships with everyone. Consequently, they may or may not be qualified to hold positions of traditional leadership. So, they may not be a fit to lead a product launch or training and development, but could be perfect to champion communicating culture.

Narrow

Depending on how many issues exist with your culture, you may need to minimize your focus to one specific area. Many companies suffer in the areas of compensation, training, work-life balance and the ability to communicate the opportunity for upward mobility. Tackling all of these matters at once is an exercise in futility. Determining the most critical area or the area to gain the quickest win is most effective.

Calculate

It's important to approach culture as a capital investment. Companies with high-level engagement experience a 28 percent increase in earnings growth and a 19 percent increase in operating income vs. an 11 percent decrease in earnings growth and a 33 percent decrease in operating income for low-level engagement. There's not a for-profit business in the world that wouldn't want to see the positive results of a highly-engaged workforce and vehemently avoid the perils of a disengaged workforce. When determining what its worth when hiring an external expert to lead the company in this effort, organizations must keep these numbers in mind.

Encounter

I could have easily decided to save a few dollars and dealt with the potential shakiness that comes with not balancing my tires, however, I want a smooth ride. Every company must determine their level of commitment to a positive culture. There are many organizations that aspire to see their organization perform at its pinnacle but never face the facts related to their poor culture. It's often easier to simply patch the major problems, as they happen, instead of investing in long-term solutions.

As I sit and ponder all of these thoughts, for the first time in forever, I'm looking forward to the morning meeting.

What I Want You to Know:

- Communicating culture requires cross-functional collaboration.

Chapter 6

- There is a significant ROI associated with a highly-engaged culture.
- Communicating culture requires BALANCE:

    - **Bridge**
    - **Analyze**
    - **Limit**
    - **Assign**
    - **Narrow**
    - **Calculate**
    - **Encounter**

CHAPTER 7

ALIGNMENT

For the first time in forever, I got home and didn't open my laptop or portfolio. The last few hours of thinking through culture caused me to consider my level of engagement at home. My ultimate vision is for my family to be happy and healthy.

To accomplish this I had done things like have "talk time" with my 13-year-old and "play time" with my youngest. I also had established a "date night" with my wife. The problem is that these had been nothing more than themed days for my family and it didn't result in us being happy or healthy.

Sure, we see each other during our routine trips to school or, twice weekly, when we actually ate at the same table, but we're certainly not highly engaged. I think I stunned everyone when I came home and immediately greeted them one-by-one with a hug and kiss. And when I asked about their day I didn't have a phone to my ear or a

Chapter 7

document in my hand. At dinner, I didn't text anyone. Although, my 13-year-old did, I never asked her to stop. I realize that they're going to have to see me consistently behave in this way.

At 5:45 a.m., I ran upstairs to shut the alarm off, because I'd been downstairs making breakfast for everyone. After I finished I left a handwritten note for each of them at their place on the table. I arrived to work at 6:45. It was a smooth ride, since I my tires had been rotated, balanced and aligned.

As we began the meeting at 7:00 a.m. sharp, Ted looked at me and said, "Mills, you have the floor." Remarkably, though I was unprepared to say anything in the meeting, I stood up with great confidence. I opened my portfolio to the notes I had jotted down while I waited for the mechanic to finish with my car. I told the group about my flat tire and that our immediate need was a SPARE. I then went on share with them that we should only move forward if we were willing to do a full ROTATION and proceed with BALANCE.

When the VP of finance sighed loud enough to cause the table to shake, I walked over to his chair. I told him how much I appreciated how he ensured that the company was fiscally responsible. It was his leadership that shielded us from

Alignment

a massive layoff during the recession and positioned the company to increase market share in the process.

I then asked him what had kept him with the organization for the last 40 years. He told a story that I had never heard before. It was about how he and the founder had met 44 years ago, in a coffee shop. At the time, he was planning to work for a firm for a few years and then start his own accounting practice, but it was something about the vision of our company that left an impression on him.

He'd told the founder to keep him in mind if the company grew, and the rest is history. When he finished sharing the story, it was clear no one in the room had ever heard it. It caused me to think about how culture becomes broken in the first place.

Unfortunately, companies who make efforts to communicate and correct culture often have no mechanism to ensure that positive culture continues. The mechanic that serviced my car the day before had also explained the importance of alignment. He said that if a car isn't aligned, it has the tendency to drift to one side and you have to turn the steering wheel away from the center position to drive straight. It could be the result of

Chapter 7

hitting a deep pothole or scoring a direct hit on a curb. Underinflated tires can also cause a vehicle to pull to one side and cause uneven wear. Tread being worn off along one edge is a sign of an alignment issue. Alignment specifications differ by vehicle, and it isn't as simple as just making sure all four wheels are pointed straight ahead.

He'd also offered that, depending on the vehicle, proper alignment involves setting the camber (inward or outward tilt of the wheels when looking head on), caster (wheel tilt front or back looking from the side) and toe-in or toe-out (looking down at the wheels from above). The adjustments are measured in fractions of an inch and require specialized alignment equipment.

It was clear that there was a passion resting in our most tenured leader that wasn't present in the rest of the leadership group, not to mention the entire organization. I turned to the board and wrote in all caps ALIGN. When considering the effort that's required in correcting and communicating positive culture, it's critical that we determine how we will ensure that our workforce is continually focusing on culture.

I could have left the shop with just patching, rotating and balancing my tires, but I ultimately would have ended up with a car that drifts while driving. I believe that many organizations create positive momentum and then drift back into the same issues. Committing to ALIGN will address this problem.

Assess

Determine the best senior leader to serve as an internal champion for the culture of your company. This person will be critical in the initial evaluation and ultimate implementation of the recommendations of the external expert. This duty is often levied on HR by default, but I encourage you to consider the best person regardless of function.

Learn

The true measure of education is improvement. Take this opportunity to learn from every problem you discover during this process. After learning everything that I now know about the importance of regularly rotating and balancing my tires, I will ensure this takes place regularly.

Invest

In times of financial constraint, efforts that address company culture are often the first to be eliminated. It is imperative that you agree to a baseline investment and protect it at all costs. It costs a lot more to operate in a failed culture than it does to maintain one that's strong. Studies show that it costs companies between 16 to 213 percent of an employee's annual salary, depending on skillset and education, to replace them.

Give

The only true way to measure culture is to provide your company with the tools and employees with the opportunities to have their voices heard. Some of these tools include absenteeism and turnover tracking software, survey platforms and weekly one-on-one meetings formats.

Neglect

Undoubtedly, there will come a time when it feels as though the company is running like a well-oiled machine. Keep in mind that even the best organizations hit potholes from time to time. Neglect the thought that positive company culture can ever be placed on cruise control. It must be monitored to ensure continuous success.

By the end of the meeting everyone was committed to start the journey. And though I was moved by the story of our VP of finance, the group elected me as the internal champion. I walked back to my office and looked out of the window at my SUV. No one would have ever known that just yesterday it was on the side of the road with a flat. I backed in today, so when I looked at my personalized name tag and thought about the upcoming journey, all I could do is laugh. I'm Ted Edward Andrew Mills, and I was born to build a solid TEAM.

What I Want You to Know:

- Correcting, communicating and continuing positive culture isn't limited to the workplace.
- Continuing culture is as critical as correcting and communicating culture.
- To ensure long-term success, you must ALIGN:
    - **Assess**
    - **Learn**
    - **Invest**
    - **Give**
    - **Neglect**

www.ingramcontent.com/pod-product-compliance
Lightning Source LLC
Chambersburg PA
CBHW050022230526
45470CB00003B/1081